CONTEMPORARY ISSUES IN INTERNATIONAL ARBITRATION

A STATUTORY AND JUDICIAL BREAKDOWN

TEJAS SATEESHA HINDER

I would like to dedicate this work to my late uncle, Mr. Gireesh Hinder, a constant driving and motivating force in my life. He rejoiced much more than I ever could at every small step of mine, both in my professional as well as personal life. My academic strife and support towards community was something he always longed for, and here's the least I could do in his name.

Love you Kaka!

Contents

Foreword

International arbitration has recently undergone a significant shift and is now a matter of intense worldwide attention. It is also presently undergoing significant challenges and criticism. In particular, the criticism of international arbitration has increased as a result of such issues. As a result, a reasonable issue about the veracity of the long-held effectiveness and widespread acceptance of international arbitration is being raised all around the world. In this work, rising threats to the practise of international arbitration are examined comprehensively.

Preface

International arbitration practise appears to be under intense worldwide scrutiny and ambiguity right now, which principally relates to the present justification of the conclusion of arbitral procedures. In addition to the illuminating evidence that international arbitration has lost ground in the field of international justice despite its continued expansion, there is also growing agreement among academics, corporations, and parties worldwide that the process has fully lost viability. First and foremost, a number of technically complex concerns connected to new difficulties are fundamentally altering the current international arbitration scene and raising questions about the current worth and legality of its operation.

Increased challenges to arbitral decisions issued by tribunals have undoubtedly grown to be a visible sign of the times, which has spread the mistrust people have for the process and result of arbitration. The commonly cited issue is that litigation-based mechanisms have replaced international arbitration, which has lost all of its effectiveness. The ultimate objectives of the parties are no longer achieved and remain valid as the purposes of international arbitration.

Acknowledgements

I would like to thank Mr. Abhijeet Kashyap, Mr. Ritik Kumar Rath, Mr. Rajneesh Prajapati, Mr. Prakarsh, Mr. Aakash Arun Rao, Mr. Lokesh Rajoria, Mr. Rahul Johari, Mr. Akanksh Deekonda, Mr. Koustav Bhattacharya and Mr. Jyotiranjan Mallick for their constant support and guidance in research as well as collation of the most relevant content for this work.

I would also like to express gratitude to my parents and relatives for their constant moral support.

CHAPTER I

CONFIDENTIALITY IN ONLINE ARBITRATIONS: SHORTCOMINGS IN THE INDIAN POSITION AND THE WAY FORWARD

<u>Background</u>

It is vital to grasp the social element of arbitration hearings in order to appreciate the need of confidentiality in any arbitration procedure. Data confidentiality is one of the most sought after advantages that arbitration delivers to the parties, amongst the mentioned list of advantages that arbitration has to give, ranging from fast, effective, and flexibility of the process. Owing to the COVID-19 pandemic, and arbitration hearings taking a virtual route, it becomes imperative to ensure extension of the protection of confidentiality to virtual hearings in order to safeguard personalised data such as login credentials of an individual, as well as documentation for such hearings saved by companies and firms, both coming under the category of firms. Such protection can hence be extended vis-à-vis the recognition of the right to privacy of such person, as the same becomes a basis to call for application of the relevant data protection statutes, ensuring a legitimate basis to claim security of the data thereinafter.

Typically, parties request protection for papers containing trade secrets or other sensitive commercial information. To avoid such disclosure of their personal information, it has been seen that the number of parties who choose Arbitration as their dispute resolution process has outnumbered those who prefer ordinary legal proceedings.

The Arbitration and Conciliation (Amendment) Act, 2019, introduced confidentiality in arbitration for the first time in India. The goal of this Amendment Act was to turn India into a centre for domestic and international arbitration. However, there is still a lot of uncertainty about data confidentiality, and arbitral institutions may be able to help in these situations by assuring stronger compliance and creating solid data security protocols.

The authors attempt to bring about the need and means for legislative inclusivity of confidentiality in arbitration in this article. The article, through methodological triangulation (doctrinal approach) identifies data protection practical needs and legal challenges in virtual arbitrations, following which through a reform oriented approach, provides a detailed insight into the legal means and need to tackle the issue of breach of confidentiality in virtual arbitrations in India through a critical examination of the existing legal position in India, indicating a way forward.

Introduction

The rise in the use of virtual hearings in arbitration processes has been attributed to the adoption of COVID-19 and the constraints it has prompted. Arbitral institutions around the world reacted quickly, issuing protocols and guidelines and hosting webinars to regulate and discuss this unique type of hearing, highlighting the similarities and differences between it and "ordinary" ones. The preceding situation highlighted a number of issues, including whether and how the requirement for confidentiality in arbitration (with a focus on commercial arbitration) can be protected when virtual hearings are used.

Confidentiality, among other issues, is a big deal breaker, making Arbitration a realistic option. For a long time, confidentiality in arbitration has been the subject of several arguments and disputes. The main challenge is whether or not arbitral procedures can comply with the system's confidentiality requirements. There are still lingering doubts about the scope and enforceability of confidentiality agreements. Due to a recent development in which arbitration is being moved to an online platform, the uncertainty associated with respecting the confidentiality clause in arbitration has become even hazier. This exacerbates the issue and creates its own set of problems.

Confidentiality in an arbitration case means that all proceedings in any session of international commercial arbitration will be conducted in camera, and that the arbitral award will not be released in the public domain without both parties' prior approval. There are two types of confidentiality: (a) confidentiality between the parties as a result of the obligation imposed on them, and (b) confidentiality with respect to the substance of the proceeding, which includes documents, hearings, and other evidence.[1]

The principle of confidentiality has always clashed with that of public interest, as well as other ideals such as mandatory disclosures to some stakeholders in a dispute, such as shareholders or insurers, when an arbitral award is challenged in court. Among the numerous benefits of confidentiality are the avoidance of unfavourable legal precedents and the reduction of the risk of compromising ongoing commercial relationships.

In general, the level of confidentiality in arbitration will vary based on a number of criteria. As a result, the effect of virtual hearings on confidentially must be assessed on a case-by-case basis rather than in broad terms. This is directly related to the ambiguity surrounding the definition of confidentiality in arbitration in the first place. While it is widely accepted that confidentiality should be imposed on the parties, the arbitral tribunal, and any arbitration institution present when applicable, whether the same should be imposed on third parties who may participate in the proceedings (such as experts or witnesses) is unclear.

When in the wrong hands, technology might jeopardise the integrity of the arbitral process. It is important to understand that all proceedings, whether online or offline, are held with the sole purpose of providing both parties with a private setting in which they can settle their disputes without fear of information being leaked.[2] It's crucial to know what technologies are being employed and to what degree they're being utilised for this. Video conferencing, emails, and file management systems are among the technologies used in online arbitration. There's also the idea of electronic filing and case management. It's tough to restrict the spread of information once it's on the internet.

There are certain actors and authorities that bear responsibility for data transmission under the international commercial framework. This is now a critical point to consider because, in the presence of various jurisdictional regimes, data transfer via online platform across borders in the presence of complicated technology becomes quite risky. With multiple layers of data transfer and high penalties for violating data protection laws, a robust and standard data protection framework is required.

Data Confidentiality and associated concerns

As a consequence of the internet's never-ending expansion, several professions and service providers have carved out a niche for themselves. The internet's development has had an impact on many facets of human existence, including regulation. The internet cleared the path for digital networking and the global e-expansion markets. The way material is handled, as well as copyright and press restrictions, has changed as a result of this. Because the internet's dynamism leads to greater international and domestic commerce, it's critical to think about how to modernise out-of-court dispute settlement. Every economy has been compelled to shutter its doors due to the present conditions put on the world economy by the COVID-19 epidemic. Not only does an individual lose a considerable amount of money, but the economy as a whole also suffers. Despite the fact that the situation has not improved, efforts are being made to resuscitate the economy in whatever manner possible. Introducing economic generators to online channels is a significant step forward in this direction.

On the other hand, the ODR mechanism was not a satisfactory success.[3] Firstly, various hardware limitations have rendered the ODR unavailable to a large segment of the population. The data prices in India are the lowest in the world; for example, in the United States, a GB of data costs INR 592, but in India, it costs just INR. 7. However, supplying low-cost data does not imply that the equipment necessary to use it are easily available. As a result, a lack of infrastructure and access to computer resources is creating a significant impediment to the growth of ODR.

The second factor is user awareness. Users' knowledge of technology and digital literacy is among the lowest among internet users worldwide. More than 90% of Indians (see here) are unaware of the extent and correct use of the internet and technology, and are fully reliant on the younger generation for even the most basic Facebook and WhatsApp setup. As a result, people's lack of understanding and mental barriers must be addressed and enhanced in order for it to be accessible to the general public.

The third issue is a scarcity of qualified specialists. Despite the fact that 10% of the Indian population is deemed digitally literate, this literacy is mostly found in the informal sector. However, India's courts and justice system work on a procedural basis, and moving them to a new platform need a well-trained and enhanced support structure. Only until the justice support system has been educated will they be able to go farther in informing people about ODR and other online court mechanisms.

Finally, one of the most important reasons is the high upfront cost of implementing approved technology, as well as the ongoing risk of data loss and device hacking. Due to the existence of aforementioned issues, the parties were discouraged from employing ODR.[4]

On the other hand, Confidentiality of proceedings indubitably remains one of the prime advantages of Arbitration. Traditionally, confidentiality would entail the protection from public disclosure of what takes place during the Arbitration.[5] The premise is to protect the interest of parties that often have to rely on critical commercial information such as profit margins, pricing policies, know-how or trade secrets etc. and other sensitive data that might potentially impact their overall public image to make their case in a proceeding.

It has widely been debated if confidentiality forms the bedrock of an arbitration proceeding. Confidentiality is affected by the parties' choice of rules governing the arbitration and also the choice of place of arbitration. Some rules tend to be more predisposed towards confidentiality requirements whereas others may not treat confidentiality as a vital requirement of the arbitration clause. Some jurisdictions, such as the United States of America, Sweden and Australia, do not treat confidentiality as an inherent part of the arbitration and hence, in absence of any explicit agreement to that effect, the parties' are not usually duty bound by any confidentiality obligation.[6] However, in jurisdictions such as the United Kingdom, confidentiality is treated as an implicit feature of the arbitration clause.[7] Therefore, even in the absence of express requirements for confidentiality there is a general obligation on the parties to maintain confidentiality of the proceedings.

It can nevertheless be said that the parties enjoy sufficient autonomy in arbitration to meticulously choose the set of laws that would favour their requirement for confidentiality. However, in the face of increasing virtualization of the proceedings, especially in the wake of the Covid-19 pandemic, it is imperative to analyze how well equipped are the existing laws to tackle the new dimensions of privacy and confidentiality that have emerged with this virtualization.

The word 'technology' clearly dominates the term 'online arbitration'. In the wrong hands, technology will jeopardise the integrity of the arbitral process. It is important to note that all hearings, whether online or offline, are conducted for the express purpose of providing all sides with a confidential setting in which they can resolve their differences without the risk of information being leaked. It's crucial to know what tools are being used and to what degree they're being used for this. Video conferencing, emails, and file management applications are among the technologies used in online arbitration. Another option is that of electronic records, which was suggested by the 2017 High-Level committee chaired by Justice B.N. Srikrishna (Retired) under Section 43K of the Act. However, Section 43K of the Arbitration Act empowers the Arbitration Council of India to keep an electronic depository of arbitral awards and other associated records in the manner provided by the rules. Once it is notified and rules are developed, it will be fascinating to examine how Section 42A, which provides for secrecy, interacts with Section 43K, which provides for depository. In order to guarantee confidentiality, the Committee advised that only Courts have access to the repository for the restricted purpose of viewing the arbitral award. This proposal, however, was rejected, and there is no mention of it in Section 43K.

According to a report released by Logic Force[8], a cybersecurity consultancy company, large corporations have been targeted by hackers. Despite the fact that they are at risk of serious publicity, most law firms are not well trained to deal with these dangers. Arbitrators and Arbitral institutions are particularly vulnerable to cybersecurity threats because they store confidential data. An instance can be the hacking of the Permanent Court of Arbitration in 2015[9], during a hearing of a sensitive maritime boundary dispute between China and the Philippines. Lastly, arbitrations may also include parties that are leading targets of cybersecurity threats, such as multinational corporations, governments or state bodies, public figures, and/or non-governmental organisations (NGOs). International arbitration cases also include verification of proof that are not available in the public domain but have the ability to affect politics and capital markets.

There are specific actors and officials who assume responsibility for data transmission under the international commercial system. This is now a critical point to remember because, in the presence of various jurisdictional regimes, data transmission via online portal across borders in the presence of complicated technologies becomes very dangerous.[10] With several layers of data transfer and high penalties for violating data privacy laws, a stable and standard data protection system is needed.

The legal status quo in India

India recently took efforts to guarantee that people's privacy is respected. In 2017, the country's Supreme Court made history by affirming the right to privacy as a fundamental right in the Puttaswamy Case[11]. Because this decision was a watershed moment in India's advancement of privacy laws, it's important to understand the timeline. During this time, the Indian government formed an expert committee led by Justice B.N. Srikrishna to develop a data security policy for the region, which eventually led to the Personal Data Protection Bill Draft. Long before this Bill was introduced in 2017, the Indian government established another committee, chaired by Justice BN Srikrishna, to review various issues related to data security in India and make clear recommendations on the standards that will underpin a Data Protection Bill.

The Personal Data Protection Bill, 2019 (hereinafter "PDP")[12] aims to regulate data privacy in India and abroad by granting territoriality to companies with a commercial relationship with India or who conduct such profiling of individuals in India. PDP refers to all sorts of personal data and is classified into two categories: sensitive and essential. Because the General Data Protection Regulation (hereinafter "GDPR")[13], a robust framework regulating data exchange and disclosure in the European Union, fails to expressly help us understand how data protection issues in other fields of law will be handled, arbitration fails to expressly help us understand how data confidentiality issues in other fields of law will be handled. The judicial system, like any other constitutionally protected entitlement, may be abused. Some fear that enacting/tightening data protection legislation may open up new avenues for "frivolous" legal action from unscrupulous parties, which might cost businesses a lot of time and money. Due to a lack of bipartisan consensus and cooperation among legislators, data privacy bills are frequently "gutted" / "watered down" by the time they are passed into law, failing to sufficiently safeguard consumer privacy rights (but still costs corporations time and money and imposes limitations of how they operate). The many personal information privacy standards imposed by separate states might impose additional constraints on businesses without a simplified federal statute. Furthermore, having each state establish its own personal data protection legislation creates the risk of conflict between state standards, making lawful data exchange difficult or impossible. ODR institutions must spend in compliance training, install new data management equipment, and maybe hire extra staff and evaluators to become/stay compliant with data protection and privacy regulations, incurring expenditures they did not have previously.

Non-personal information is exempt from the GDPR, which specifies that disclosure of personal information may be justified for reasons such as consumer protection, public safety, law enforcement, rights enforcement, cybersecurity, and fraud prevention. Furthermore, the GDPR does not apply to domain names registered by American registrars and registries for US registrants. It also doesn't apply to domain name registrants who aren't "natural people," such as organisations, businesses, or other legal entities. Despite this, because the GDPR's rules are so unclear and the possible penalties are so significant, parties such as ICANN use voluntary filtering. Proponents of the GDPR are likely to have contributed to the perception that the GDPR encourages procedures like the Temporary Specification.

Without effective measures to foster education or innovation, the GDPR and CCPA maintain the status quo, rewarding the largest players while punishing small and medium-sized businesses and deceiving individuals into believing they have better privacy when they are really being placed at danger. The bureaucratization of data protection does not result in the creation of a natural right to privacy. Having an ever-increasing number of regulators and rules governing data does not make a person safer. Regulation maintains the status quo; it does not promote system or user knowledge development.

The GDPR has a significant unintended consequence of undermining the transparency of the international mechanisms and architecture that manage the internet. The Internet Corporation for Assigned Names and Numbers (ICANN) has published a Temporary Specification that permits registries and registrars to suppress WHOIS data that was previously needed to be made public, presumably to comply with the GDPR. This might stymie attempts to tackle illegal activities online, such as identity theft, cyberattacks, online espionage, intellectual property theft, fraud, illegal drug sales, human trafficking, and other crimes, and it isn't even required under the GDPR.

This may have given you a hint that India currently lacks data privacy regulations, let alone a specialised arbitration code. The 1996 Arbitration and Conciliation Act, as important as it is for party control and confidentiality, is plagued by statutory issues. Despite the fact that the Act was updated to include Sections 42A and 43K, the public has yet to be notified. As a consequence, there is a great deal of uncertainty regarding how data security and, by extension, confidentiality may be addressed in the arbitral procedures now underway in India.

The non-obstante provision in Section 42A of the amended Act states that all parties in the trials must maintain confidentiality, with the exception of the prize, which must be disclosed if the award is to be enforced and implemented. The rights of any party desiring to bring sensitive material from arbitration to a court are now in doubt as a result of this statute.

The law dealing to Confidentiality Clubs has been characterised by constantly shifting jurisprudence over the last few years. Given that only the Delhi High Court has established some conditions for their formation and that there is no statutory provision to recognise these clubs, it has become more of an emerging judge-made legislation.

A detailed examination of the above-mentioned passed orders reveals that the membership of Confidentiality Clubs is still unclear. The *Transformative Learning Solutions*[14]and *Genentech Inc.*[15]orders, which enable the inclusion of parties and internal experts, differ from previous orders that only permitted advocates and external experts to be members of the clubs. It would be interesting to observe how the courts create these groups in the future to safeguard the secret of the records.

The constitution of these clubs is expected to be expanded in the coming days to include litigation in other areas such as arbitration, competition law, and data protection. Given the prevalence of these clubs in court processes, having a structured, controlled statutory framework becomes vitally crucial. Given that this is one of the exceptions to the open justice principles, a framework is required to strike a compromise between preserving sensitive information and ensuring open justice access.

Another important factor to consider is the participation of other parties in the arbitral process, which may be reliant on sensitive material discovered during the arbitration in cases of consolidation of multiple arbitral proceedings or joinder of parties to an initiated or ongoing arbitration.

In Vidya Drolia and Ors. v. Durga Trading Corporation[16], the Supreme Court of India allowed third parties to assert their reference in arbitration proceedings by demonstrating their level of interest, implying that such reference proceedings may necessitate the disclosure of sensitive arbitration details. The Court delved deeper into the issue of subject-matter arbitrability and the scope and ambit of the Court's jurisdiction while dealing with an application made under Section 8 or 11 of the Arbitration and Conciliation Act, 1996, while dealing with an application made under Section 8 or 11 of the TPA.

As a consequence, Indian courts will need to specify the criteria for releasing sensitive information in court proceedings, as well as consider the interests of parties seeking an exemption under Section 42A of the Act. Other nations, such as Singapore and the United Kingdom, are currently debating this legal problem. The conflict of interest that arises when providing information for the public good persists; however, since the public good is an exception to the clause, a balancing method is necessary. One of the aims of the Arbitration and Conciliation (Amendment) Act, 2019 (hereinafter "2019 Amendment")[17] was to create the Arbitration Council of India as an autonomous regulatory body for all arbitrations held in India. It also wants the Arbitration Council of India (hereinafter "ACI") to settle on data fiduciaries and data principles as part of the PDP Bill. Since the PDP bill determines what a data fiduciary is, it is unclear whether the data fiduciary is an arbitrator or an arbitral institution. Even while such provisions try to protect data security, they fall short of solving the situation at hand, hence India demands a data privacy protocol immediately.

<u>Shaping Indian Arbitral Institutions: A lesson from International Arbitral Institutions</u>

Institutional Arbitrations have always stood as a tall example of ensuring uniformity and providing a definite structure for arbitration proceedings through their own set of rules. These rules usually provide flexibility with regard to the procedural measures to be adopted in the smooth conduct of arbitral proceeding.[18] They have especially stood out in the Covid times because of their quick adaptability and ability to handle virtual hearings and e-filings.

Despite the new challenges faced in terms of security and confidentiality, arbitral institutions have been producing guidance to best address these challenges. Best practices would see parties, their representatives and the arbitrator agreeing on a set of reasonable precautions to be taken with regard to cybersecurity, privacy and data protection at the start of arbitration proceedings to ensure an appropriate level of security for the case.

Institutionalization of arbitration in India is still at a budding stage and the need to strengthen Institutional Arbitration in India has acquired more relevance than ever due to the restrictions posed by the pandemic. The Amendment Act, 2019 setup the Arbitration Council of India for grading arbitral institutions with an attempt to strengthen institutional arbitration in India. Presently there are about 35 arbitral institutions in India such as the Indian Council of Arbitration ("ICA"), the Delhi International Arbitration Centre ("DIAC"), the Mumbai Centre for International Arbitration ("MCIA"), to name a few. But only a handful of them actively partake in arbitration and have continued to do so during the pandemic. There is a significant lot that India can learn from the international institutional practice in terms of fortifying its infrastructure to accommodate the need of the hour.

Some of the international institutional rules already provided a mechanism for remote hearing and aid of digital support for conducting arbitration even before this pandemic induced digital revolution was brought about in the realm of Arbitration. For instance, the Hong Kong International Arbitration Centre (HKIAC) had introduced provisions centered on the use of technology for document submission and conduction of arbitration proceeding three years ago in 2018.[19] The International Chamber of Commerce ("ICC") too already provided for the 'use of telephone or video conferencing for procedural and other hearings where attendance in person is not essential and use of virtual tools that enables online communication among the parties, the arbitral tribunal and the Secretariat of the Court.'[20] In fact, Rule 24(4) of the ICC Rules also provides that the case management conference may be held virtually over telephone or video call.

Others seem to have adapted to the exigent and special requirements of the current times by modelling new rules to support virtual arbitration in pandemic times. The ICC and SIAC are currently successfully facilitating arbitration proceedings involving parties located in various jurisdictions by way of video conferencing, and have released guidelines and advisories for the conduct of arbitrations in these times. The ICC released its 'Guidance Note on Possible Measures Aimed at Mitigating the Effects of the COVID-19 Pandemic' ("ICC COVID19 Guidance") in April 2020.[21] SIAC, on the other hand, has addressed issues pertaining to the virtual conduct of arbitration through the SIAC-COVID FAQs available on its website.[22] The CIArb released a detailed guidance note on Remote Dispute Resolution Proceedings with specific provisions on confidentiality and security.[23] In India, the Mumbai Centre for International Arbitration (MCIA) has also continued to operate virtually and provided parties with the option to conduct remote arbitrations using its audio-video capabilities.[24]

With this particular indispensability of digitization of arbitration by Institutional Rules, confidentiality has acquired a new flavour with some special issues such as data protection and cyber security that need to be addressed. The International Institute for Conflict Prevention & Resolution has recognized the paramount importance of confidentiality in virtual proceedings and has empowered the tribunal to terminate the proceedings if it feels that confidentiality is compromised during the process.[25] It also prohibits access to the live video and/or audio feed of the proceeding other than disclosed Participants. All participants are advised to avoid the use of open or public WiFi networks and required to join through wired or secure wifi networks, which may include the use of a reliable virtual private network ("VPN").[26]

The CIArb guidance has taken meticulous care even with respect to the surroundings in which the participants shall be seated during the virtual proceeding. Article 6.3 of the guidance note requires the sound proofing of the setting where possible, and also requires the positioning of the camera in a fashion that allows sufficient visibility to eliminate the possibility of the presence of undisclosed non-participating individuals in the surrounding.[27] This addresses the concern regarding the presence of a third party in the room where the witness or expert is supposed to be giving the evidence. Other than the stipulated provisions of institutional rules, recourse shall also be taken to instruments such as the ICCA-NYC Bar-CPR Protocol on Cybersecurity in International Arbitration (2020 Edition) and the IBA Cybersecurity Guidelines 2018 to address cyber security concerns. The former particularly sets out information and cyber security risks factors in an arbitration proceeding and provides guidance in determining reasonable cyber security measures for a virtual arbitration.[28]

The Indian Institutional framework can take inspiration from the international developments in Institutional arbitration across the globe and homogenise them to prepare an appropriate mix suited for the Indian palate. In this regard, the IAF Protocol on Virtual Hearings for Arbitrations released in 2020 seems be a decent attempt at a holistic guidance on virtual proceedings.[29] It provides, inter alia, the use of end to end encrypted communication channels and networks. Special emphasis is also to data processing and storage in those servers whose location is identifiable and attracts the applicable laws. It also recommends reference to the ICCA-NYC Bar-CPR Protocol on Cybersecurity in International Arbitration for ensuring adequate cyber security measures. However, in the long run, to avoid unnecessary delays and potential disagreement over applicable rules, it is advisable that the arbitral institutes incorporate their own specific provisions in their institutional rules itself to which the parties would have subscribed while choosing the administering institution.

The Way Forward

Confidentiality under Arbitration was for the very first time introduced in India by way of The Arbitration and Conciliation (Amendment) Act, 2019. The objective behind bringing this Amendment Act was to develop India into a hub of domestic and international arbitration. No doubt that a ground breaking attempt was made by Indian Legislature by bringing Sections 42A and 43K via the 2019 Amendment. Both these provisions were introduced with the hope to the course of confidentiality under arbitration. However, the outline of Section 42A and the exception provided thereunder remains arbitrary and vague in nature. Moreover, the regulations for data security by ACI are yet to see face of the dawn.

The provision makes no mention of confidentiality requirements for a case taken to court. Furthermore, by overriding sections that are in contradiction with it, the non-obstante provision introduced to the amendment further confuses the legislation. This provision does not recognise any customary exceptions, such as "public interest" and "justice." The PDP bill, however, has no mention of arbitration and does nothing to address the gap left by COVID-19's virtual arbitrations. When it comes to personal security, things are also a little foggy, and arbitration agencies may be able to help by maintaining greater uniformity and developing stringent data privacy policies.

COVID-19 has presented a plethora of new issues, but it also provides an excellent opportunity for arbitration to consider the future of information technology and the places where the two could be linked. Virtual arbitration may become the new status quo. As a result, specialised law, such as data protection, is a necessary/unavoidable requirement of the hour. According to the publishers, PDP may be amended to contain and allude to arbitration-ruled data privacy issues.

Even existing forms of courts have been relocated to the internet portal as a result of the worldwide pandemic, and there has also been an increase in online arbitration hearings with the goal of enhancing productivity and cutting expenses. People are increasingly adopting data as a critical mode of communication as the digital economy grows at an exponential rate. India not only needs a robust mechanism to fill in the gaps in its data security procedure created by the PDP Bill, but it also has to do it as fast as feasible. The government has a legal incentive to prevent all forms of cyber-attacks and maintain improved security levels.

It is currently a legislative necessity in India to require Indian courts to specify the parameters of releasing sensitive information in court cases and to consider the needs of parties requesting an exception under Section 42A. The conflict of interest that emerges when disclosing details for the public good persists; however, because the public good is an exception to the clause, a balancing mechanism is required.

The challenges with regard to proceedings confidentiality are amplified without a proper data management policy in place. The PDP Bill makes no attempt to close these gaps. It's also unclear whether data protection measures would be judged mandatory or susceptible to voluntary consensus in consent-based ad hoc arbitrations. Although it is unclear whether such restrictions would be adopted in the near future, it is vital to emphasise cybercrime's growing threat. This could lead to huge financial losses for all parties involved, as well as jeopardise the prosecutions' credibility.

In India, it's unclear how data privacy, and thus confidentiality, will be addressed. Moving toward arbitration agencies that will maintain stronger security requirements and establish stringent data preservation protocols in order to ease the myriad problems that may arise as a result of data breaches and cyber-attacks could be the answer. The ACI's laws may include a data privacy protocol to address these concerns.

There is now a regulatory opportunity to connect the PDP Bill's data protection goals with the (to-be-drafted) norms of the ACI. On the other hand, the ambiguity surrounding Section 42A's limitations on confidentiality requirements necessitates quick court intervention.

[1] Jose Rosell, *Confidentiality and arbitration*, Croatian Arbitration Yearbook, Vol. 9 (2002).

[2] Richard C. Reuben, *Confidentiality in Arbitration: Beyond the Myth*, 54 U. Kan. L. Rev. 1255 (2006).

[3] The NITI Aayog Expert Committee on ODR, *Designing the Future of Dispute Resolution: The ODR Policy Plan for India*, NITI Aayog (October, 2021), available at: https://www.niti.gov.in/sites/default/files/2021-11/odr-report-29-11-2021.pdf.

[4]*Id.*

[5] Marlon Meza-Salas (DLA Piper), *Confidentiality in International Commercial Arbitration: Truth or Fiction?*, Kluwer Arbitration Blog (Sep. 23, 2018), available at: http://arbitrationblog.kluwerarbitration.com/2018/09/23/confidentiality-in-international-commercial-arbitration-truth-or-fiction/.

[6] Esso Australia Resources Ltd. v. Hon. Sydney James Ploughman (1995), 128 ALR 391; United States v. Panhandle Eastern Corp., 118 F.R.D. 346 (Del. 1988); Bulgarian Foreign Trade Bank Ltd v. AI Trade Finance Inc, T-1881-99, Swedish Sup Ct (2000).

[7] Ali Shipping Corp. v. Shipyard Trogir, [1998] 2 All ER 136.

[8] Logic Force Consultancy, *Annual Study on Cybersecurity* (2016), available at: https://www.logicforce.com/

reports/detail/cybersecurity-q1.

[9] Jason Healey and Anni Piiparinen, *Did China Just Hack the International Court Adjudicating Its South China Sea Territorial Claims?*, The Diplomat (Oct.27, 2015) available at: https://thediplomat.com/2015/10/did-china-just-hack-the-international-court-adjudicating-its-south-china-sea-territorial-claims/.

[10] UNCTAD, *Data protection regulations and international data flows: Implications for trade and development, United Nations Publication,* UNCTAD/WEB/DTL/STICT/2016/1/iPub, available at: https://unctad.org/system/files/official-document/dtlstict2016d1_en.pdf (2016).

[11] K.S. Puttaswamy v. Union of India, (2017) 10 SCC 1.

[12] The Personal Data Protection Bill, 2019, Bill No. 373 of 2019 (India).

[13] Regulation (EU) 2016/679 of the European Parliament and of the Council, *EU General Data Protection Regulation (GDPR)* (2016).

[14] Transformative Learning Solutions Pvt. Ltd. & Ors. v. Pawajot Kaur Baweja & Ors., CS(COMM) 817/2018, IA No. 5583/2018 (u/O XXXIX R-1&2 CPC) & IA No.6193/2018 (u/S 151 CPC).

[15] Genentech Inc. and Ors. v. Drugs Controller General of India and Ors., CS(OS) 3284/2015.

[16] Vidya Drolia v. Durga Trading Corporation, 2020 SCC OnLine SC 1018.

[17] The Arbitration and Conciliation (Amendment) Act, 2019, No. 52, Acts of the Parliament, 2019 (India).

[18] Report of the High Level Committee to Review the Institutionalisation of Arbitration Mechanism in India, Department of Legal Affairs, available at: https://legalaffairs.gov.in/sites/default/files/Report-HLC.pdf (Jul. 30, 2017).

[19] Hong Kong International Arbitration Centre, *HKIAC Administered Arbitration Rules*, 2018, Article 13.1.

[20] International Chamber of Commerce, *ICC Arbitration Rules*,2021 ,Appendix IV, available at: https://iccwbo.org/dispute-resolution-services/arbitration/rules-of-arbitration/.

[21]International Chamber of Commerce, *ICC Guidance Note on Possible Measures Aimed at Mitigating the Effects of the COVID-19 Pandemic,* 2020, available at: https://iccwbo.org/content/uploads/sites/3/2020/04/guidance-note-possible-measures-mitigating-effects-covid-19-english.pdf.

[22] SIAC Covid-FAQs, available at: https://siac.org.sg/faqs/36-featured-template/advanced-shortcodes/frequently-asked-questions-faq/657-siac-covid-19-frequently-asked-questions-faqs.

[23] Chartered Institute of Arbitrators, *Guidance Note on Remote Dispute Resolution Proceedings,* 2020, available at: https://www.ciarb.org/media/9013/remote-hearings-guidance-note_final_140420.pdf.

[24] Alok Jain, Dhruv jain, *Arbitration in the time of COVID-19,* BAR AND BENCH, (May 26, 2021, 20:08 PM), https://www.barandbench.com/columns/arbitration-in-the-time-of-covid-19 .

[25] Institute for Conflict Prevention and Resolution (CPR), *Annotated Model Procedural Order for Remote Video Arbitration Proceedings,* 2020 available at: https://www.cpradr.org/resource-center/protocols-guidelines/model-procedure-order-remote-video-arbitration-proceedings.

[26]*Annotated Model Procedural Order for Remote Video Arbitration Proceedings, CPR,* 2020 available at: https://www.cpradr.org/resource-center/protocols-guidelines/model-procedure-order-remote-video-arbitration-proceedings.

[27] Chartered Institute of Arbitrators, *Guidance Note on Remote Dispute Resolution Proceedings,* 2020, available at: https://www.ciarb.org/media/9013/remote-hearings-guidance-note_final_140420.pdf.

[28] Principle 6 read with Schedule B, International Council for Commercial Arbitration, New York City Bar Association, and International Institute for Conflict Prevention and Resolution

(CPR), *Protocol on Cyber security in International Arbitration, 2020,* available at:https://cdn.arbitration-icca.org/s3fs-public/ document/media_document/icca-nyc_bar- cpr_cybersecurity_protocol_for_international_arbitration_- _print_version.pdf

[29] Indian Arbitration Forum, *IAF Protocol on Virtual Hearings for Arbitrations,* 2020, available at: https://indianarbitrationforum.com/wp-content/themes/iaf/ assets/IAF-Protocol-on-Virtual-Hearings-for-Arbitrations- Oct-2020.pdf

ASYMMETRIC JURISDICITION CLAUSES VIS-À-VIS DISPUTE RESOLUTION IN THE UK: WHAT IN 2022 IN THE AFTERMATH OF BREXIT?

Background

In an asymmetric jurisdiction, the parties submit to the jurisdiction of one or more designated courts, but some parties' submissions are exclusive while others are not. Therefore, provisions of an asymmetric jurisdiction clause ("AJC") might be interpreted as either granting a certain Court exclusive jurisdiction over a dispute or delegating that authority to that Court.

Currently, the freedom to choose any Court to hear the dispute by the party with more extensive jurisdiction raises a few key questions, including whether such a Court will be *stricto sensu* 'any Court' or a Court of 'competent jurisdiction' and how the capability of a Court in a transnational dispute with multiple domestic procedural rules will be determined.

The Brussels Regulation (Recast) and the 2005 Hague Convention are two of the main pieces of EU law that an AJC is based on. However, as a result of Brexit, the United Kingdom can no longer rely on the Brussels legislation after December 2020. Therefore, Parties are prevented from using the Hague Convention. In the event that the UK does not ratify the 2007 Lugano Convention, parties are attempting to establish jurisdiction and reciprocal recognition of judgments under the Hague Convention on Choice of Court Agreement.

Asymmetric clauses are most likely recognised under the Lugano Convention as exclusive choice of court agreements because the United Kingdom ("UK") has applied to accede to this Convention, which is broadly comparable to the Brussels Recast

Regulation and to which the UK government has applied to accede. It is still uncertain whether or when the UK will really accede to it because all signatories must agree, and the European Union ("EU") hasn't done so yet.

Asymmetric jurisdiction provisions are acceptable under the Brussels Recast Regulation as an exclusive jurisdiction clause, according to English courts' rulings in the instances of Etihad Airways PJSC and Commerzbank Aktiengesellschaft. However, given that the Brussels Recast Regulation no longer applies in the UK as a result of Brexit, this only has immediate impact for actions that begin on or before December 31, 2020.

There are certain areas of doubt in the current system for exclusive jurisdiction clause enforcement in the UK and across the EU, but overall, it is reliable enough to be employed.

This article looks at the current position of the UK in regard to AJCs, covering the issues surrounding enforceability and examines a feasible road ahead.

The current position of the UK and the enforcement conundrum

Uncertainty surrounds the Hague Convention's applicability to jurisdiction agreements made prior to January 1, 2021. The EU and its member states have suggested that they may not, but the UK has stated that it will implement such accords as if the Hague Convention applied. Uncertainty and concurrent legal actions may result from this. Additionally, temporary remedies like an injunction will not be subject to execution under the Hague Convention. The parties may decide to restate their agreement at this time to make sure it is covered by the Hague Convention in order to prevent this confusion.

Contracting parties will no longer be able to depend on treaty-based enforcement of their English judgements throughout the EU, Switzerland, Iceland, and Norway as of January 1, 2021, without the Hague Convention, as these countries are not signatories to the Hague Convention.

In general, it is likely that decisions made in business disputes other England will be upheld in member nations, and vice versa. Since the courts could recognise and enforce each other's judgements until fairly recently, there is no reason to believe that since Brexit the various courts' rulings are any less secure. However, recognition won't happen automatically. It could be necessary to start new legal action to enforce the verdict. Before determining whether to file procedures, it will likely take considerably longer and cost more money. It may also be essential to pay for local enforcement guidance. Potential claimants may be discouraged from pursuing their claims by the uncertainty.

Possibility of Optional Arbitration Clauses

Similar to asymmetric jurisdiction agreements, optional arbitration clauses are untested in many countries, therefore it is unclear what stance the courts there will likely adopt. The courts of some jurisdictions may decline to enforce an optional arbitration clause or any judgement or award made in reliance thereon, either on the basis of public policy considerations or on the ground that it is a conditional agreement and thus in some way violates Article II of the New York Convention, even though such clauses are permissible under English law, as in the case of NB Three Shipping case.

In the ZAO Russian Telephone Company case, a London arbitration clause with a unilateral option to litigate contained in an English law governed contract was found to be invalid by the Supreme Arbitrazh Court of Russia. Interestingly, in France, notwithstanding the Rothschild case, such optional arbitration clauses have been upheld in the case of Société Générale SA case.

The Way Forward

In accordance with the Brussels Convention, the Lugano Convention, the common law, or some combination of them, English courts may stay their legal actions in favour of another nation decided upon by the parties. The ways in which that agreement is expressed and the permitted exceptions may differ slightly from the existing situation.

Likewise, EU Member States will undoubtedly continue to accept exclusive jurisdiction clauses designating the English courts, whether the UK is a Brussels Convention state, a Lugano Convention state, or simply a non-Member State within the scope of the Brussels Regulation. Instead of a global convention, this may be accomplished through their own domestic conflict of law laws.

If the UK just joins the other non-member states, it may result in more room for delay strategies. However, the UK will probably once more be allowed to deploy anti-suit injunctions if its negotiating position is outside the Brussels rules. By the Brussels Regulation, as mentioned above, this potent tool to force compliance with an exclusive jurisdiction provision was substantially taken out of the English courts' legal toolbox.

The UK may ask for a special status as a non-Member State under the Brussels Regulation system if it wants a situation that is similar to the status quo. The Lugano Convention might be a close substitute if this is not politically possible, maybe because it would necessitate acknowledging the Court of Justice of the European Union's ongoing supremacy. However, the EU might not be open to letting the UK stick with the current system or anything similar. The UK might then elect on its own to ratify the Hague Choice of Courts Convention and rely on its past participation in the Brussels Convention. This results in a system that incorporates a reasonable amount of reciprocity, particularly for agreements involving exclusive jurisdiction.

It is anticipated that the domestic legislation concerning the recognition of judgments in EU member states will be enforced if the UK is unable to establish a trustworthy reciprocal arrangement that recognises and implements AJCs. Without the Brussels Recast Convention or its equivalent, it is conceivable that many EU member states will uphold English judgments. This is not guaranteed, and international rulings that are implemented for consistency are probably just going to be superficial.

Uncertainty over the post-Brexit strategy is also brought on by the uneven attitude taken by EU nations to date. In any case, this ambiguity highlights how crucial it is to make sure covenants to pay are added moving forwards to local law security papers. This precaution would not, however, totally eliminate the requirement to determine the terms of the principal credit arrangement under the applicable legislation, which is typically English law. Determining whether a proper default has actually happened and, if so, whether that default authorises the lenders to 'enforce their local law security are only two examples of such requirements.

To be clear, it should be underlined that these concerns with cross-border security enforcement will only materialise if a legal challenge to financial documents is successful and results in the cross-border enforcement of security. Under financing documents, parties are allowed to settle problems amicably and regularly, with judicial action serving as a last resort. Another situation where the lack of the Recast Brussels Regulation or any successor agreement will have no bearing is when security is frequently implemented outside of court without the necessity for any kind of legal action or procedure.

Although the use of unequal jurisdiction provisions reflects market practise, the latest Loan Market Association Guidelines and the new post-Brexit framework may make this conventional method more problematic than helpful. This problem could be solved by symmetric jurisdiction provisions because they are enforceable under the Hague Convention. The benefits of being able to employ the Hague Convention by choosing such symmetric provisions over depending on the various laws and legal systems in the 27 EU nations may outweigh the drawbacks of using symmetric jurisdiction clauses.

CHAPTER III

DISCOVERING THE NEED TO EMPOWER ARBITRAL TRIBUNAL TO ORDER FOR INTERIM COSTS: A NEED FOR RECOGNIZING FINANCIALLY DEPENDENT PARTIES RELIANT ON THIRD PA

Introduction

An application for disclosure of third-party funding and order for security for legal cost should be accepted. Firstly, disclosure should be made pursuant to Rule 27 of the SIAC Rules, 2016 and SIAC Practice Note on Arbitrator Conduct in Cases Involving External Funder, dated March 31, 2017, which mandated the disclosure of third party funding. Also, providing for disclosure at the outset of the proceeding would also protect the integrity of the administering institution as it can avoid the potential conflict of interest between the members of the tribunal and the third party funder. Secondly, tribunals have the power to order security for costs as an interim measure under SIAC Rules, 2016 and UNCITRAL Model Law, 1985 without amendment. Further, the conditions for ordering security of cost as interpreted in line with international arbitration practice are fulfilled that is to say presence of third-party funding and merits of the claims.

This article looks at the need and means to empower arbitral tribunals to order for interim costs in cases of third party funding vide the SIAC Rules, by an impact-based analysis of the advantages that it poses as lex arbitri in this regard. In doing so, the article also uncovers and attempts to resolve the debate around pre-requisites in this regard which play a major contributing factor.

Model Lex Arbitri for Consideration: Why and What under SIAC Rules?

Rule 27(j) of the SIAC Rules, 2016 provides for additional power to the tribunal to "order any party to provide security for legal or any other costs in any manner the tribunal thinks fit".[1] Further Article 17 of the UNCITRAL Model Law, 1985 without amendment provides for the power of the tribunal to order interim measures as "the tribunal may require any party to provide appropriate security in connection with such measure".

The tribunal should refrain from ordering security for costs because international arbitration practice and scholarly opinion take an adversarial stance on the matter. There is an absence of any court or arbitral cases or legal scholars arguing that security for costs is not an interim measure. On the contrary, many authorities agree that security for costs can be ordered as an interim measure. Security for costs is an anticipatory measure to facilitate the enforcement of a costs award by preserving assets for that purpose, which makes it an interim measure.

Since the SIAC Rules are also silent on ways to estimate the reasonableness of legal costs, arbitrators have wide discretion to fix the amount in light of all the circumstances of the case.

In short, security for costs is an interim measure covered by the SIAC Rules, 2016 and the UNCITRAL Model Law, 1985 for the above-mentioned reasons. Thus, a tribunal set up with the SIAC rules as the lex arbitri has the power to order security for legal costs.

The Debate around Pre-Requisites

Although the SIAC Rules, 2016 bestow the power to order security for costs, they do not offer any guidance on under which circumstances the power should be exercised. Instead, the tribunal should turn to international arbitration practice for considering the conditions for ordering interim measures.

The use of third party funding can be justified for security for costs on the basis that one side may likely be impecunious (hence the need for third-party funding) and will not be able to satisfy any costs award, and the third party funder who is not a party to the arbitration has no obligation to satisfy any costs award and will be able to walk away if unsuccessful.

The SIAC Practice Note provides that 'The tribunal may take into account the existence of any external funder in apportioning the costs of the arbitration, and an appointed tribunal may take into account the involvement of an external funder in ordering . . . that all or a part of the legal or other costs of a Disputant Party be paid by another Disputant Party. These provisions confirm that the tribunal may take into account funding arrangements when apportioning costs of the arbitration and awarding costs to a funded party.

Gavan Griffith QC, in his capacity as tribunal member in investor-state arbitration, has suggested that, once third party funding is revealed, "the onus is cast on the Claimant to disclose all relevant factors and to make a case why security for costs should not be made".

An act of not disclosing the involvement of a third-party funder and further denying the existence of one is proof enough to establish the intent and financial inabilities, so as to satisfy the claims in the future. A similar approach has been suggested by others, according to which, "where a party appears to lack assets to satisfy a final costs award but is pursuing claims in an arbitration with the funding of a third party, then a strong prima facie case for security for costs exists".

Conclusion

The strict application of rules of evidence is at odds with the intended informality of arbitration. All that is required is that the material ... [be] sufficiently persuasive to permit a rational belief to be formed that, if ordered to do so, the corporation would be unable to pay the costs of that party upon disposal of the proceedings.

The tribunal in the case of Oilex A.G. vs. Mitsui & Co. (USA) stated that the opposing party's financial health is a major factor to consider when contemplating a security request because the payment of a substantial sum of money is at the root of security for costs orders (ordering security because 'plaintiff has no assets or is out of business'). Orders for security are the standard method of protecting a party against the other's potential inability to pay costs.

To conclude, the tribunal should find that it has the power to order security for costs as an interim measure under the applicable law and rules. The conditions for the order of security for legal costs are set in the international arbitration practices.

CHAPTER IV

JURISDICTION OF AN ARBITRAL TRIBUNAL AND AMICABLE SETTLEMENTS AS PRE-ARBITRAL OBLIGATIONS: AN ANSWER TO WHAT SHOULD TAKE PRECEDENCE

Introduction

Determination of jurisdiction of an arbitral tribunal on the basis of fulfilment of existing pre-arbitral obligations agreed upon by parties to the arbitration has been a precedent followed in arbitrations. This allows for contesting the jurisdiction of the arbitral tribunal when such obligations have not been fulfilled. However, when clauses determining such obligations are vaguely worded or not capable of being construed, their fulfilment becomes non-mandatory.[1]

Arbitration cases have overseen the possibility of directing parties to interpret such clauses that are deemed to be vague, and agree on a common ground and means for fulfilment of the obligation (which would be in line with the principle of party autonomy), where the language of the clause is unclear as to the specific means to be undertaken, but the pith and substance behind it can be construed.

This article attempts to address the Conundrum of fulfilment of Amicable Settlements as pre-Arbitral Requirements in cases of vague but reasonably determinable pre-Arbitral Obligation Clauses for creation of jurisdiction of constituted Arbitral Tribunal. This is done by considering surrounding factors such as existence of consent to such pre-arbitral obligations when part of the contractual agreement, intent of parties and an arbitral tribunal's capacity to rule over its own jurisdiction.

<u>Voluntary consent to arbitrate: A factor to consider</u>

The parties to an arbitration initiated as agreed under a contract, by way of entering into a contract consented to the agreement to arbitrate as international arbitration agreements are creatures of contract.[2] As held in a well-reasoned award of the ICC, "an arbitral tribunal should construe the validity and scope of an arbitration clause in accordance with the general principles of the interpretation of contracts, i.e., seeking the real and common intent of parties, based on the wording of the clause, and the principle of confidence or good faith."[3]

Further, applying the UNCITRAL Model Law, a well-reasoned Singapore Appellate decision concluded, "An arbitration agreement should be construed like any other commercial agreement. The fundamental principle of documentary interpretation is to give effect to the intention of the parties as expressed in the document. A commercially logical and sensible construction was to be preferred over another that was commercially illogical."[4]

National courts and arbitral tribunals have also frequently applied the rules that the specific prevails over the general.[5] As one authority concluded, "an age-old precept of contract interpretation requires that agreements be interpreted as a whole to give meaning to all terms, but when provisions conflict so that all cannot be given full weight, the more specific clauses are deemed to reflect the parties' intentions – a specific provision controls a general one,"[6] while a frequently-cited arbitral award held that, "under the rule of interpretation *lex specialis* derogate *legi generali* the more specific provision takes precedence over the more general one."[7]

In a substantial majority of all jurisdictions, national law provides that international arbitration agreements should be interpreted in light of a "pro-arbitration" presumption.[8] Derived from the policies of leading international arbitration conventions and national arbitration legislation, and from the parties" likely objectives, this type of presumption provides that a valid arbitration clause should generally be interpreted expansively and, in cases of doubt, extended to encompass disputed claims. That is particularly true where an arbitration clause encompasses some of the parties' disputes and the question is whether it also applies to related disputes, so that all such controversies can be resolved in a single proceeding (rather than in multiple proceedings in different forums).

In the words of one award applying the UNCITRAL Rules, there is a "tendency...not only to a non-restrictive but even to an expansive view of international arbitration [clauses]."[9] Or, as another tribunal held, interpretation of an arbitration agreement "goes beyond the requirements of a strict literal interpretation. To the contrary, when the parties insert an arbitration agreement in their contract, one should presume that their intent was to establish an effective machinery for the settlement of disputes."[10]

Amicable settlement as pre-arbitral steps not mandatory: Beyond mere ambiguity of clauses allowing questioning the tribunal's jurisdiction

In Walford v. Miles, in which Lord Ackner held that a bare agreement to negotiate was unenforceable as a mere 'agreement to agree'.[11] The issue presented to the Court of Appeal was whether mediation was a binding condition precedent to the commencement of arbitration. The Court held that it was not, as it did not contain clear language to that effect and did not define the obligation to mediate with sufficient certainty. In particular, the Court held that the multi-tier clause "did not set out any defined mediation process, nor does it refer to the procedure of a specific mediation provider." Rather, it "contained merely an undertaking to seek to have the dispute resolved amicably by mediation" and "no provision was made for the process by which that was to be undertaken."[12] Accordingly, the court ruled that mediation was not a jurisdictional condition precedent to arbitration.[13]

Similarly, in Tang Chung Wah & Anor v. Grant Thornton International Ltd.[14], the contract at issue contained a multi-tier dispute resolution clause that provided that prior to commencing arbitration, the parties were required to refer disputes to conciliation for one month, after which the parties were required to refer disputes to a panel of three individuals identified in the clause. The clause made clear that until those steps were undertaken "no party may commence any arbitration procedures in accordance with this Agreement."[15] The claimant in that case commenced an arbitration against the respondent without fulfilling the pre-arbitral steps, and the respondent asked the tribunal to dismiss the claim for lack of jurisdiction. The tribunal found that it had jurisdiction, so the respondent sought to have this determination set aside by the High Court (Chancery Division). Ultimately, the High Court upheld the tribunal's ruling, and held that the pre-arbitral steps in the multi-tier clause did not constitute binding conditions precedent to the commencement of arbitration, because they did not contain clear language to that effect and did not adequately specify the form in which the prearbitral steps should proceed.

In the 2014 decision of BG Group Plc v. Republic of Argentina[16], the United States Supreme Court took the position that a failure to comply with pre-arbitral steps set out in multi-tier clauses do not deprive an arbitral tribunal of jurisdiction to adjudicate a dispute, without clear language to the contrary.

Likewise, in an ICC case from 2001[17], the contract at issue required that the parties undertake efforts to negotiate disputes prior to submitting them to arbitration. In that case, the claimant commenced arbitration against the respondent without making any effort to negotiate, and the respondent consequently challenged the jurisdiction of the tribunal. In its defence, the claimant contended that negotiations would have been futile and urged the tribunal to accept jurisdiction. The tribunal rejected the Respondent's application and asserted jurisdiction over the dispute. It relied in large measure on its finding that there would have been little prospect of settlement had they carried out negotiations prior to arbitration. In particular, the tribunal stated: "The arbitrators are of the opinion that a clause calling for attempts to settle a dispute amicably are primarily expression of intention, and must be viewed in the light of the circumstances. They should not be applied to oblige the parties to engage in fruitless negotiations or to delay an orderly resolution of the dispute. Accordingly, the arbitrators have determined that there was no obligation on the claimant to carry out further efforts to find an amicable solution, and that the commencement of these arbitration proceedings was neither premature nor improper."[18]

Kompetenz-Kompetenz: The overriding factor

Jurisdictional questions themselves are considered capable of settlement by arbitration, pursuant to agreement by the parties.[19] Under these circumstances, an arbitrator's determination on his or her own authority will be final. The parties' agreement transforms the jurisdictional difference into a disputed question of fact or law, whose substantive merits the litigants submit to final determination by an arbitrator.[20]

The UNCITRAL Model gives the arbitral tribunal an explicit right to determine its own jurisdiction in the form of a "preliminary" award, subject to challenge on a request from a party within thirty days.[21]

The principle of Kompetenz-Kompetenz is distinct from, but intersects functionally with, the notion that an arbitration agreement can be operationally detached from the main contract in which it is found. Often conceptualized as a matter of separability, the principle that an arbitration clause possesses contractual autonomy permits the arbitrators to do their job, notwithstanding what their award might say about the validity of the contract in dispute. The separability doctrine gives the arbitration clause the status of a contract autonomous from the principal agreement in which it is encapsulated.[22]

[1] S. Kumar Construction Co. & Anr v. Municipal Corporation of Greater Bombay, Appeal No.914 of 2003

[2] Gary B. Born, International Commercial Arbitration (2d Ed, Kluwer Law International 2014) pp. 1317 - 1403.

[3] Interim Award in ICC Case No. 7929, XXV Y.B. Comm. Arb. 312, 317 (2000).

[4] Insigma Tech. Co. Ltd v. Alstom Tech. Ltd, [2009] 3 SLR(R) 936, ¶¶30, 33 (Singapore Ct. App.).

[5] Dr. Horst Reineccius v. Bank for Int'l Settlements, Partial Award in PCA Case of 22 November 2002, XXVIII Y.B. Comm. Arb. 100, 130 (2003).

[6] Karnette v. Wolpoff & Abramson, LLP, 444 F.Supp.2d 640, 646 (E.D. Va. 2006).

[7] Final Award in ICC Case No. 5946, XVI Y.B. Comm. Arb. 97, 102 (1992).

[8] William W. Park, 'The Arbitrator's Jurisdiction To Determine Jurisdiction, I. Introduction: The Limits Of Language', In Albert Jan Van Den Berg (Ed), International Arbitration 2006: Back To Basics?, ICCA Congress.

[9] Wintershall AG v. Government of Qatar, Partial Ad Hoc Award of 5 February 1988, 28 Int'l Legal Mat. 795, 811 (1989).

[10] Award in ICC Case No. 9759, discussed in GrigeraNaón, Choice-of-Law Problems in International Commercial Arbitration, 289 Recueil des Cours 9, 89-90 (2001).

[11] Walford v. Miles, [1992] 1 All ER, at 460.

[12] Sulamerica CIA Nacional de Seguros v. EnesaEngenharia, [2012] EWCA Civ 638, ¶ 36.

[13]Id.

[14] Tang Chung Wah & Anor v. Grant Thornton International Ltd., [2012] EWHC 3198 (Ch).

[15]Id., ¶ 27.

[16] BG Group PLC v. Republic of Argentina, 572 (2014) (slip op.).

[17] ICC Case No. 8445, Final Award, XXVI Y.B. Comm. Arb. 167 (2001).

[18]Id., p. 169.

[19] Veijo Heiskanen, *Dealing with Pandora: The Concept of 'Merits' in International Commercial Arbitration*, 22 Arb. Int'l (2006, no. 4) pp. 597-611.

[20]*Supra Note* 7.

[21] Model Arbitration Law of the United Nations Commission on International Trade Law, art. 16 (1985).

[22] Gary B. Born, International Commercial Arbitration (2d Ed, Kluwer Law International 2014) pp. 1317 – 1403.

CHAPTER V

ENFORCEMENT OF EMERGENCY ARBITRATION AWARDS: DONE YET UNDONE?

Introduction

At times, parties want immediate relief due to the possibility of irreparable damage in the future. They have two solutions at hand: to approach the court for interim relief or wait for the formation of the Arbitral Tribunal. But since both the processes are time taking, parties cannot go with either of them since that may cause financial damage to either of them. This is where the aspect of emergency arbitration has been critically important for the past few years in helping the parties to obtain adequate remedy in a short period of time. Emergency arbitration helps acts as an immediate relief to maintain the status quo between the parties.

Even though the concept of emergency arbitration has come in handy and has proved to be an appropriate substitute for the interim relief given by courts, it still suffers from a substantial number of irregularities and uncertainties. One of the criticisms of emergency arbitration awards has been the enforcement aspect. The article mainly deals with the impediments in the way of enforcing Emergency Awards by the parties and how this problem can be rectified to save the aggrieved party to suffer from unnecessary and irreparable damage.

Ambiguity over Enforcement of Emergency Awards

Earlier, the parties had no option but to approach the courts or wait for the formation of the Arbitral Tribunal whenever they wanted immediate relief in a dispute. As these means were time consuming and compromised the rights of the parties, a new form of remedy was derived in order to provide quick relief to the aggrieved in an efficacious and effective manner within a span of 5 to 15 days.

Several Arbitration Institutions have incorporated provisions concerning pre-arbitral interim measures in their rules, thereby officially recognizing the mechanism of Emergency Arbitration. Out of all the International Arbitration Institutions, International Chamber of Commerce ('ICC') was the first to offer parties an out-of-court mechanism for urgent interim relief. The ICC rules "enable parties that have so agreed to have rapid recourse to a person (called a "Referee") empowered to make an order designed to meet the urgent problem at issue, including the preservation or recording of evidence". The concept of interim relief was then adopted by the UNCITRAL Model Law in 2006. Other global institutions which have amended their rules to provide parties to have recourse to interim measures before the beginning of the Arbitration process include American Arbitration Association, Singapore International Arbitration Centre, Hong Kong International Arbitration Centre, Netherlands Arbitration Institute etc. These steps taken by the International Institutions to reinforce Emergency Arbitration provide the parties with a plethora of benefits including autonomy, immediate relief and less strain on courts.

But all of the advantages of Emergency Arbitration are usually cancelled out by the lack of enforcement measures provided under various systems. The general rule is that the awards passed under Emergency Arbitration are binding on the parties taking part in the arbitration process. But the subsequently formed Arbitral Tribunal is not bound by the award passed by the Emergency Arbitrator, enabling the former to either reconsider, modify or annul the award. Thus, the award passed by the Emergency Arbitrator is usually not considered final by the party against whom it has been passed making it difficult for the other party to enforce the same.

One of the reasons for the ambiguity over the enforcement of emergency awards is the inability of the legislatures of countries to recognize emergency arbitration in their municipal statutes, due to which the aggrieved party cannot approach the court under the Arbitration Laws to enforce the award passed by the emergency arbitrator. This in turn refutes the whole purpose of emergency arbitration to provide instant and immediate relief to the parties to save them from loss.

Only a handful of states have made amendments to their national legislations to enable the enforceability of Emergency Arbitrator's decisions. One of the countries to take steps towards this is Singapore, who made an amendment to its Arbitration Law in order to bring Emergency Arbitrators within the definition of 'Arbitral Tribunals'. This would result in the enforcement of the Emergency Arbitration Awards in the same manner as the awards given by Arbitral Tribunals. Hong Kong and Netherlands have done the same thing, which lets the courts to grant leave to enforce awards provided by Emergency Arbitrators.

India

India does not have a robust Emergency Arbitration system due to the absence of the same in the Arbitration and Conciliation Act, 1996. The inclusion of this mechanism was recommended by the 246th Law Commission report in 2014, which stated that the definition of 'Arbitral Tribunal' under Section 2 (d) needs to be expanded to include Emergency Arbitrator. The recommendation was ignored by the parliament as no inclusive changes with respect to the same were made in the Arbitration and Conciliation Act, 2015.

The awards passed by the Emergency Arbitrators are usually not recognized by the Indian Courts. This further complicates the process, making it difficult for the parties to get the appropriate remedy within days, ultimately defeating the whole purpose of the mechanism. This leaves them with the only option to enforce the award under Section 9 of the Arbitration and Conciliation Act.

In the landmark case of *HSBC PI Holdings (Mauritius) Limited v. Avitel Post Studiouz Limited and Ors.*, the Bombay High Court enforced the award passed under Emergency Arbitration by granting similar reliefs to the Petitioner under Section 9 of the Arbitration Act.

A completely opposite judgement was pronounced by the Delhi High Court in *Raffles Design International India Private Limited & Ors. v. Educomp Professional Education Limited & Ors.*, in which the court refused to enforce the award given by the Emergency Arbitrator but agreed to pass any relief if the Petitioner approached the court independently under Section 9 of the Arbitration Act.

These decisions clearly depict the difference in approach of various courts, which adds even more ambiguity to the status of enforcement of Emergency Arbitration in the country. The provisions related to Emergency Arbitration in the Mumbai Centre for International Arbitration ('MCIA') rules is not enough to provide adequate relief to the parties. Unless the same is not incorporated in the Arbitration Act, jurisprudence with respect to Emergency Arbitration would remain ambiguous, giving rise to even more instances wherein the parties suffer.

<u>Conclusion</u>

The overall legal framework seems to be uncertain towards the enforceability of awards granted by Emergency Arbitrators. Even though the international arbitration institutions have taken a step forward to recognize and enforce the cases arising out of emergency arbitration, the same won't be effective unless the states make amendments in their respective national Arbitration laws. The importance of emergency arbitration cannot be undermined given the huge number of cases in which parties have resorted to it, hoping to get a favourable decision. This has often been thwarted by the persisting uncertainty over the nature and enforceability of measures issued by Emergency Arbitrators.

CHAPTER VI

DILEMMA SURROUNDING ABSENCE OF COMMUNICATION IN APPOINTMENT OF ARBITRATION TO BE INITIATED: IS AN INTERMEDIATE PATRY–BINDING ADJUDICATION NECESSARY?

Introductory Remarks

An impact based assessment of Section 11(6) of the Arbitration and Conciliation Act (hereinafter "the Act"), was brought about by The Delhi High Court on Tuesday, 09/02/2021, in its adjudication of Oyo Hotels and Homes (P) Ltd. v. Rajan Tewari[1], in which it held an appointment of an arbitrator to be unilateral and hence non-est, due to the Petitioner not responding to the Respondent's communication, indicating such appointment, made in furtherance of an unambiguous arbitration agreement between the parties.

This article looks at the issue of such non-response in light of Party Autonomy, due to party autonomy being intrinsic to the process of arbitration, and mere technical non-compliance not being a sufficient and significant ground to oust something as substantial as party autonomy. In doing so, the article puts forward a potential mechanism through which such appointment and hence resolution of the dispute could take place, and at the same time an attempt to ensure party autonomy to the highest extent is made.

A look down on Party Autonomy

Party autonomy is widely considered the guiding principle in determining the procedure to be followed in an international commercial arbitration.[2] Party autonomy is deemed to be respected if the procedures that the parties consented to are implemented.[3] Exclusivity and harmony are two terms often used to describe the process of Arbitration.[4] The concept of party autonomy provides for the freedom to determine the persons entitled to participate in the arbitration proceedings.[5]

An agreement to settle a dispute by arbitration, by appointing an arbitrator hence reflects upon the willingness of parties to select a competent and neutral, yet mutually amicable compositor to adjudicate upon the dispute. Hence, resorting to take away such autonomy through engagement of judicial appointment of such arbitrator takes away the essence and purpose of such freedom, and all the more turns out to be arbitrary, considering the fact that competent judicial authorities are statutorily empowered to direct either or both parties to respond to notices of initiation of proceedings, appointments, etc.[6] Hence, what seemingly comes up here is the need for an intermediate adjudication, directing the non-responding party to convey their assent or dissent to communications for the purposes of appointment.

<u>Mandating the non-responsive party to adhere to the arbitration agreement</u>

Having clarified the importance of party autonomy, it becomes imperative to analyse how to ensure it to the maximum extent while considering this issue. With unilateral appointment of arbitrators barred by the law,[7] competent courts should direct parties not responding to such notices of appointment within fifteen days, as suggested by the Department of Legal Affairs[8] as indicated by in the absence of an inability to do so, i.e. the situation not legally exempting parties from being bound to take part in arbitrations (which includes reasons such as initiation of moratorium periods due to party being declared insolvent), to do so. This ensures a fair opportunity afforded to the parties, to amicably decide on the arbitrator to adjudicate the dispute, which in addition to party autonomy, fulfils the underlying principle behind arbitration as a dispute resolution mechanism, which is the parties' freedom to contract.[9] This principle is so deeply rooted inside the process of arbitration that procedural efficacy and economic considerations can be side stepped for it to prevail.[10]

<u>Non-compliance to time limits: An overriding factor?</u>

A question that does arise is the presence of time limits, and actions to be taken in case the same is defaulted, so as to ensure speedy resolution of disputes. With substantial reduction of the time to 15 days for response, and the court empowered to mandate responses, on a persuasive note, it is to be understood that adherence to time limits is a procedural stipulation[11]. The standard for the enforcement of procedural requirements is that of substantial compliance.[12] As long as the actual step mentioned in the arbitration rules has been taken, errors in lieu of technical noncompliance, such as minor delays in filing documents, which cause no prejudice to the other parties[13], are not grounds for dismissal of a claim[14].

A counter-contention that may arise here is whether these procedural stipulations of time to revert may infringe upon party autonomy, but since such stipulation of fifteen days is being imposed for default by one party to such arbitration, which affects the other party attempting to have an arbitrator appointed and initiate proceedings for resolution of the dispute, i.e. party autonomy is not affected here since the question is that of a mutual reciprocating obligation, and not that of freedom.

[1] Oyo Hotels and Homes (P) Ltd. v. Rajan Tewari, Arb. P. 424 of 2020.

[2] Piero Bernardini, *Transnational Rules in International Commercial Arbitration*, ICC Pub, p.115 (1998).

[3] Klaus P. Berger, *Party Autonomy in International Commercial Arbitration*, American Review of International Arbitration, Vol. 4, p.7 (1993).

[4] Bharat Aluminium Co. v. Kaiser Aluminium Technical Services Inc., Civil Appeal 3678 of 2007 (28 January

2016); Martin Hunter, Nigel Blackaby, Constantine Partasides, *Law and Practice of International Commercial Arbitration*, Sweet & Maxwell: London, 4th ed., (2004).

[5] Renusagar Power Company Ltd. v. General Electric Company, AIR 1985 SC 1156; Stavros Brekoulakis, *The Relevance of the Interests of Third Parties in Arbitration: Taking a Closer Look at*

the Elephant in the Room 113 (4) P. S. L. R. 1165, 1166 (2013).

[6] Arbitration and Conciliation Act, sec. 25 (1996); Walter Bau Ag. v. MCGM, (2015) 3 SCC 800.

[7] Perkins Eastman Architects DPC v. HSCC (India) Ltd., Arbitration Application No.32 OF 2019.

[8] Department of Legal Affairs, *Report of the High Level Committee to Review the Institutionalism of Arbitration Mechanism in India* (Jul. 30, 2017), available at: https://legalaffairs.gov.in/sites/default/files/Report-HLC.pdf

[9] Thomas E. Carbonneau, *The Exercise of Contract Freedom in Making of Arbitration Agreements* 36 V. J. T. L. 1189, 1189-96 (2003).

[10] Arjun Gupta, Sahil Kanuga & Vyapak Desai, *Blessed Unions in Arbitration- An Introduction to Joinder and Consolidation in Institutional Arbitration* 4(2) I. J. A. L. 134, 136 (2016).

[11] David D. Caron, Stephan W. Schill, Abby Cohen Smutny, and Epaminontas E. Triantafilou, *Practising Virtue*

Inside International Arbitration, Oxford University Press, 17 (2015).

[12] Wimmer v. Richards, 330 Md. 52 (1993); Mitcherling v. Rosselli, 304 Md. 363 (1985); Regina v. Soneji and Bullen, HL 21 Jul 2005.

[13] O'Neill v. Jacobs, 890 P.2d 1092 (1995).

[14] Hoirup v. Empire Airways, 69 Wn. App. 479 (1993).